Precut Quilts

Perfect for beginners – or anyone who enjoys fast and easy projects – these fun quilts all rely on precut fabrics for convenience and variety. Pull out your charm packs, jelly rolls, and fat quarters and get inspired!

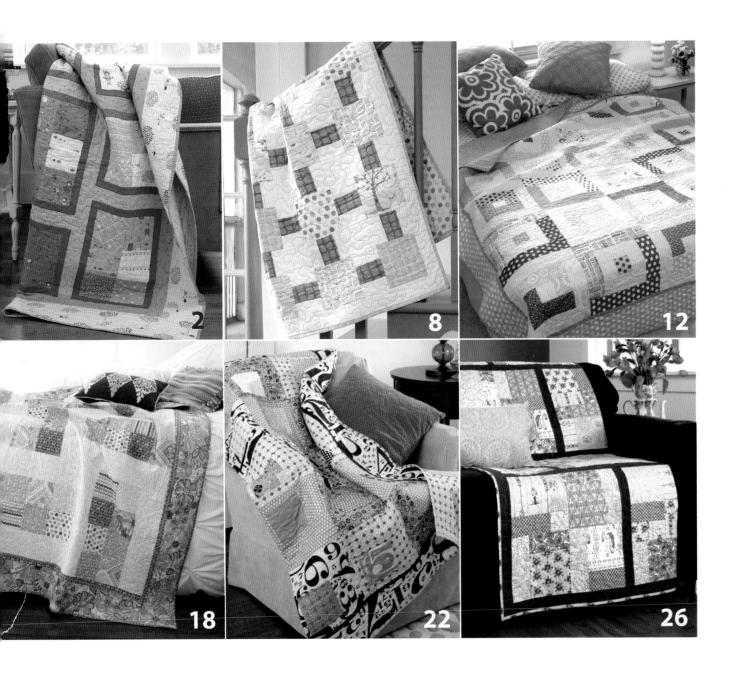

LEISURE ARTS, INC. • Little Rock, Arkansas

an apple a day

Finished Quilt Size: 52" x 56½" (132 cm x 144 cm)
Finished Large Block Size: 11" x 15½" (28 cm x 39 cm)
Finished Small Block Size: 11" x 11" (28 cm x 28 cm)

SHOPPING LIST

Yardage is based on 43"/44" (109 cm/112 cm) wide fabric with a usable width of 40" (102 cm). Charm squares are 5" x 5" (13 cm x 13 cm).

- ☐ 1 Charm Pack or 42 squares 5" x 5" (13 cm x 13 cm)
- ☐ ⅝ yd (57 cm) of red solid fabric
- ☐ ¾ yd (69 cm) of teal print fabric
- ☐ ⅞ yd (80 cm) of white print fabric
- ☐ 3⅝ yds (3.3 m) of fabric for backing
- ☐ ½ yd (46 cm) of fabric for binding
- ☐ 60" x 64½" (152 cm x 164 cm) piece of batting

CUTTING THE PIECES

Follow **Rotary Cutting**, page 31, to cut fabric. Cut all strips from the selvage-to-selvage width of the fabric. Borders and sashings are cut exact length. All measurements include 1/4" seam allowances.

From red solid fabric:
- Cut 12 strips 1½" wide. From these strips, cut:
  - 12 **small block side borders** 1½" x 9½".
  - 12 **small block top/bottom borders** 1½" x 11½".
  - 6 **large block side borders** 1½" x 14".
  - 6 **large block top/bottom borders** 1½" x 11½".

From teal print fabric:
- Cut 9 strips 2½" wide. From these strips, cut:
  - 6 **horizontal sashings** 2½" x 11½".
  - 4 **vertical sashings** 2½" x 42", pieced as needed.
  - 2 **top/bottom sashings** 2½" x 41½", pieced as needed.

From white print fabric:
- Cut 5 strips 5½" wide. From these strips, cut:
  - 2 **side borders** 5½" x 46", pieced as needed.
  - 2 **top/bottom borders** 5½" x 51½", pieced as needed.

From fabric for binding:
- Cut 6 **binding strips** 2¼" wide.

MAKING THE BLOCKS

Follow **Machine Piecing** and **Pressing**, page 32, to make quilt top. Use 1/4" seam allowances throughout.

1. Divide charm squares by color. Sort squares into groups of 4 squares for each Small Block and 6 squares for each Large Block. Pay attention to direction of any novelty print motifs if you would like them positioned upright. Once you are pleased with your groups, sew squares together to create 6 **Unit 1's** and 3 **Unit 2's**.

Unit 1 (make 6)

Unit 2 (make 3)

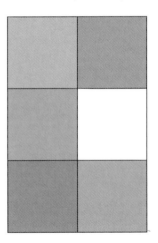

Sew 1 **small block side border** to each side of 1 Unit 1. Sew **small block top/bottom borders** to top and bottom of 1 Unit 1 to make a Small Block. Make 6 Small Blocks.

Small Block (make 6)

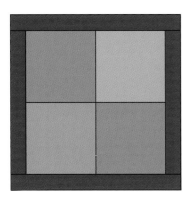

3. Sew 1 **large block side borders** to each side of 1 Unit 2. Sew **large block top/bottom borders** to top and bottom of Unit 2 to make a Large Block. Make 3 Large Blocks.

Large Block (make 3)

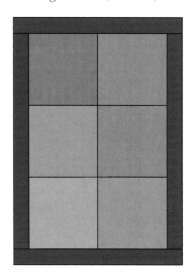

ASSEMBLING THE QUILT TOP

*Refer to **Assembly Diagram** to assemble the vertical rows. Again, pay attention to the direction of any novelty print motifs.*

1. Sew 1 large block, 2 small blocks, and 2 **horizontal sashings** together to make a vertical row. Make 3 vertical rows.

Assembly Diagram

2. Matching centers and corners, sew vertical rows and **vertical sashings** together. Repeat to sew **top** and **bottom sashings** to quilt top.
3. In same manner, sew **side borders** to quilt top and then sew **top** and **bottom borders** to quilt top.

COMPLETING THE QUILT

1. Follow **Quilting**, page 33, to mark, layer, and quilt as desired. Quilt shown is quilted with an all-over meandering pattern.
2. Follow **Making a Hanging Sleeve**, page 35, if a hanging sleeve is desired.
3. To piece binding strips, use the diagonal seams method *(Fig. 1)*.

Fig. 1

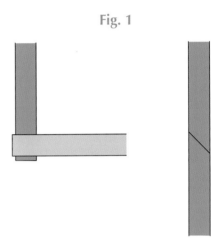

4. Matching wrong sides and raw edges, press strip in half lengthwise to complete binding.
5. Follow **Attaching Binding**, page 36, to bind quilt.

backyard fun

Finished Quilt Size: 42" x 58" (107 cm x 147 cm)
Finished Block Size: 3" x 5" (8 cm x 13 cm)

SHOPPING LIST

Yardage is based on 43"/44" (109 cm/112 cm) wide fabric with a usable width of 40" (102 cm). Fat quarters are approximately 22" x 18" (56 cm x 46 cm).

- ☐ 5 assorted fat quarters
- ☐ ½ yd (46 cm) of grey print fabric
- ☐ 1½ yds (1.4 m) of white print fabric
- ☐ 3¾ yds (3.4 m) of fabric for backing
- ☐ ½ yd (46 cm) of fabric for binding
- ☐ 50" x 66" (127 cm x 168 cm) piece of batting

CUTTING THE PIECES

*Follow **Rotary Cutting**, page 31, to cut fabric. When cutting from yardage, cut all strips from the selvage-to-selvage width of the fabric. When cutting from fat quarters, cut all strips parallel to one long edge. Borders are cut exact length. All measurements include $^1/_4$" seam allowances.*

From *each* assorted fat quarter:
- Cut 2 strips $5^1/_2$" wide. From these strips, cut a total of 7 **large squares** $5^1/_2$" x $5^1/_2$".

From grey print fabric:
- Cut 6 **strips** $2^1/_2$" wide.

From white print fabric:
- Cut 3 strips $3^1/_2$" wide. From these strips, cut 24 **small squares** $3^1/_2$" x $3^1/_2$".
- Cut 12 **strips** 2" wide.
- Cut 2 **side borders** $2^1/_2$" x $53^1/_2$", pieced as needed.
- Cut 2 **top/bottom borders** $2^1/_2$" x $41^1/_2$", pieced as needed.

From fabric for binding:
- Cut 6 **binding strips** $2^1/_4$" wide.

MAKING THE BLOCKS

*Follow **Machine Piecing** and **Pressing**, page 32, to make quilt top. Use $^1/_4$" seam allowances throughout.*

1. Sew 1 grey print **strip** and 2 white print **strips** together to make a **Strip Set**. Make 6 Strip Sets. Cut across Strip Sets at $3^1/_2$" intervals to make a total of 58 **Blocks**.

Strip Set (make 6)

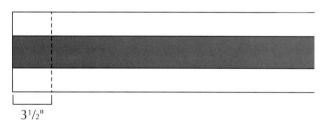

$3^1/_2$"

Block (make 58)

ASSEMBLING THE QUILT TOP

1. Sew 5 assorted **large squares** and 4 Blocks together to make **Row A**. Make 7 Row A's.

Row A (make 7)

2. Sew 5 **Blocks** and 4 **small squares** together to make **Row B**. Make 6 Row B's.

Row B (make 6)

3. Sew **Row A's** and **Row B's** together to make **Quilt Top Center**.
4. Matching centers and corners, sew **side borders** to Quilt Top Center. Repeat to sew **top** and **bottom borders** to Quilt Top Center.

COMPLETING THE QUILT

1. Follow **Quilting**, page 33, to mark, layer, and quilt as desired. Quilt shown is quilted with an all-over meandering pattern.
2. Follow **Making a Hanging Sleeve**, page 35, if a hanging sleeve is desired.
3. To piece binding strips, use the diagonal seams method *(Fig. 1)*.

Fig. 1

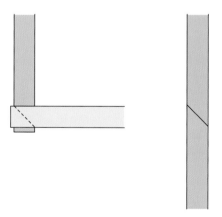

4. Matching wrong sides and raw edges, press strip in half lengthwise to complete binding.
5. Follow **Attaching Binding**, page 36, to bind quilt.

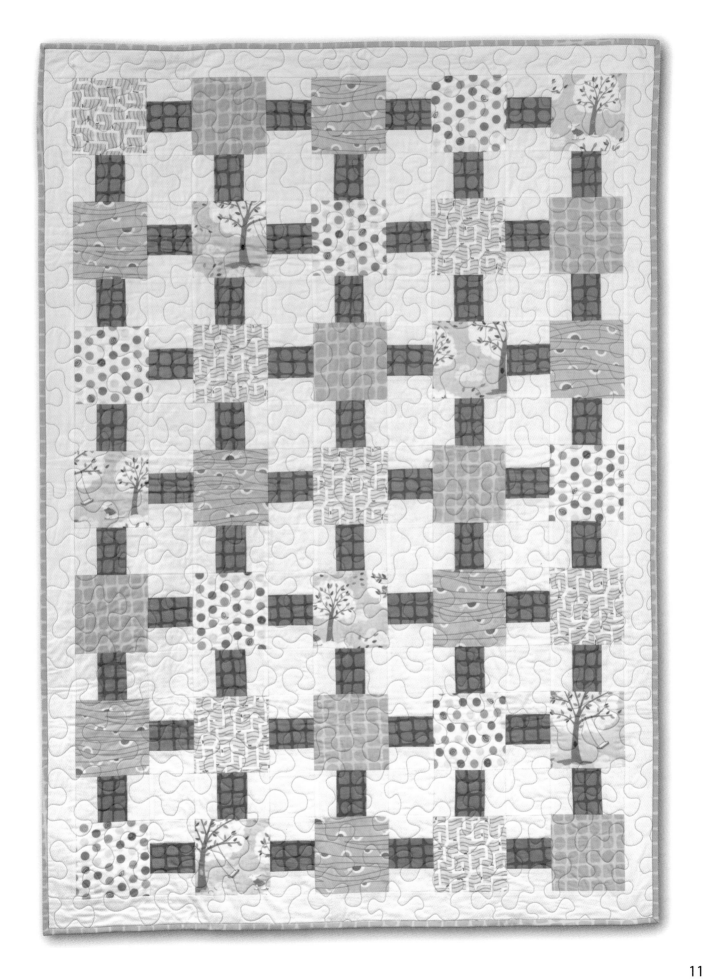

coming home

Finished Quilt Size: 62" x 72" (157 cm x 183 cm)
Finished Block Size: 10" x 10" (25 cm x 25 cm)

SHOPPING LIST

Yardage is based on 43"/44" (109 cm/112 cm) wide fabric with a usable width of 40" (102 cm). Fat quarters are approximately 22" x 18" (56 cm x 46 cm). A jelly roll includes 40 strips $2^1/2$"w x width of fabric.

- ☐ 1 Jelly Roll
- ☐ $1^7/8$ yds (1.7 m) of cream solid fabric for blocks
- ☐ $^1/4$ yd (23 cm) of grey solid fabric for inner borders
- ☐ $1^1/4$ yds (1.1 m) of yellow polka dot fabric for outer borders
- ☐ $4^1/2$ yds (4.1 m) of fabric for backing
- ☐ $^5/8$ yd (57 cm) of fabric for binding
- ☐ 70" x 80" (178 cm x 203 cm) piece of batting

CUTTING THE PIECES

*Follow **Rotary Cutting**, page 31, to cut fabric. Cut all strips from the selvage-to-selvage width of the fabric. Borders are cut exact length. All measurements include $1/4$" seam allowances.*

From jelly roll strips:
- Cut 15 assorted **square A's** $2^1/2$" x $2^1/2$".
- Cut 30 assorted sets of 1 **square B** $2^1/2$" x $2^1/2$" and 1 **short rectangle C** $2^1/2$" x $6^1/2$".
- Cut 30 assorted sets of 1 **short rectangle C** $2^1/2$" x $6^1/2$" and 1 **long rectangle D** $2^1/2$" x $10^1/2$".

From cream solid fabric:
- Cut 3 strips $2^1/2$" wide. From these strips, cut 45 **square B's** $2^1/2$" x $2^1/2$".
- Cut 10 strips $2^1/2$" wide. From these strips, cut 60 **short rectangle C's** $2^1/2$" x $6^1/2$".
- Cut 10 strips $2^1/2$" wide. From these strips, cut 30 **long rectangle D's** $2^1/2$" x $10^1/2$".

From grey solid fabric:
- Cut 2 **side inner borders** 1" x $60^1/2$", pieced as needed.
- Cut 2 **top/bottom inner borders** 1" x $51^1/2$", pieced as needed.

From yellow polka dot fabric:
- Cut 4 **outer borders** $5^1/2$" x $61^1/2$", pieced as needed.

From fabric for binding:
- Cut 8 **binding strips** $2^1/4$" wide.

MAKING THE BLOCKS

*Follow **Machine Piecing** and **Pressing**, page 32, to make quilt top. Use $1/4$" seam allowances throughout.*

1. Sew 1 print **square A** and 2 cream **square B's** together to make **Unit 1**. Make 15 Unit 1's.

Unit 1 (make 15)

2. Sew cream **short rectangle C's** to top and bottom of Unit 1 to make **Unit 2**. Make 15 Unit 2's.

Unit 2 (make 15)

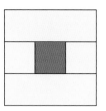

3. Sew assorted print **short rectangle C's** to sides of Unit 2 to make **Unit 3**. Make 15 Unit 3's.

Unit 3 (make 15)

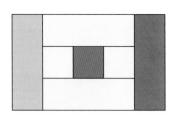

Using long rectangles that match short rectangles used in Step 3, sew **long rectangle D's** to top and bottom of Unit 3 to make **Block A**. Make 15 Block A's.

Block A (make 15)

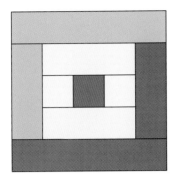

Sew 1 cream **square B** and 2 assorted print **square B's** together to make **Unit 4**. Make 15 Unit 4's.

Unit 4 (make 15)

Using short rectangles that match squares used in Step 5, sew **short rectangle C's** to top and bottom of Unit 4 to make **Unit 5**. Make 15 Unit 5's.

Unit 5 (make 15)

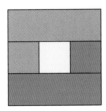

7. Sew cream **short rectangle C's** to sides of Unit 5 to make **Unit 6**. Make 15 Unit 6's.

Unit 6 (make 15)

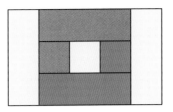

8. Sew cream **long rectangle D's** to top and bottom of Unit 6 to make **Block B**. Make 15 Block B's.

Block B (make 15)

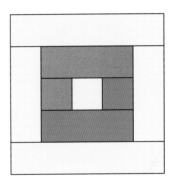

ASSEMBLING THE QUILT TOP

1. Beginning and ending with a Block A, sew 3 Block A's and 2 Block B's together to make **Row A**. Make 3 Row A's.

Row A (make 3)

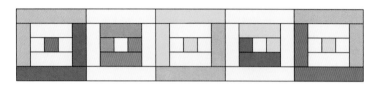

2. Beginning and ending with a Block B, sew 2 Block A's and 3 Block B's together to make **Row B**. Make 3 Row B's.

Row B (make 3)

3. Alternating Rows, sew Row A's and Row B's together to make **Quilt Top Center**.
4. Matching centers and corners, sew **side inner borders** to Quilt Top Center. Repeat to sew **top** and **bottom inner borders** to Quilt Top Center.
5. In same manner, sew 1 **outer border** to each side of Quilt Top and then sew remaining **outer borders** to top and bottom of Quilt Top.

COMPLETING THE QUILT

1. Follow **Quilting**, page 33, to mark, layer, and quilt as desired. Quilt shown is quilted with an all-over meandering pattern.
2. Follow **Making a Hanging Sleeve**, page 35, if a hanging sleeve is desired.
3. To piece binding strips, use the diagonal seams method *(Fig. 1)*.

Fig. 1

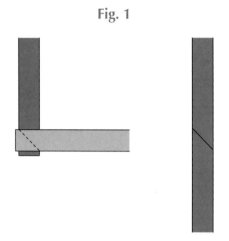

4. Matching wrong sides and raw edges, press strip in half lengthwise to complete binding.
5. Follow **Attaching Binding**, page 36, to bind quilt.

floating 8

Finished Quilt Size: 67" x 85" (170 cm x 216 cm)
Finished Block Size: 18" x 18" (46 cm x 46 cm)

SHOPPING LIST

Yardage is based on 43"/44" (109 cm/112 cm) wide fabric with a usable width of 40" (102 cm). Fat quarters are approximately 22" x 18" (56 cm x 46 cm). Charm squares are 5" x 5" (13 cm x 13 cm)

- ☐ 8 assorted fat quarters or 96 charm squares
- ☐ 1⁷⁄₈ yds (1.7 m) of cream solid fabric for blocks
- ☐ ³⁄₈ yd (34 cm) of grey print fabric for inner borders
- ☐ 1³⁄₈ yds (1.3 m) of large floral print fabric for outer borders
- ☐ 5¹⁄₄ yds (4.8 m) of fabric for backing
- ☐ ⁵⁄₈ yd (57 m) of fabric for binding
- ☐ 75" x 93" (191 cm x 236 cm) piece of batting

CUTTING THE PIECES

*Follow **Rotary Cutting**, page 31, to cut fabric. When cutting from yardage, cut all strips from the selvage-to-selvage width of the fabric. When cutting from fat quarters, cut all strips parallel to one long edge. Borders are cut exact length. All measurements include $1/4$" seam allowances.*

From *each* fat quarter:
- Cut 3 strips 5" wide. From these strips, cut 12 **squares** 5" x 5".

From cream solid fabric:
- Cut 12 strips 5" wide. From these strips, cut 24 **rectangles** 5" x $18^1/2$".

From grey print fabric:
- Cut 2 **side inner borders** $1^1/2$" x $72^1/2$", pieced as needed.
- Cut 2 **top/bottom inner borders** $1^1/2$" x $56^1/2$", pieced as needed.

From large floral print fabric:
- Cut 2 **side outer borders** $5^1/2$" x $74^1/2$", pieced as needed.
- Cut 2 **top/bottom outer borders** $5^1/2$" x $66^1/2$", pieced as needed.

From fabric for binding:
- Cut 9 **binding strips** $2^1/4$" wide.

MAKING THE BLOCKS

*Follow **Machine Piecing** and **Pressing**, page 32, to make quilt top. Use $1/4$" seam allowances throughout.*

1. Sew 8 **squares** together to make **Unit 1**. Make 12 Unit 1's.

Unit 1 (make 12)

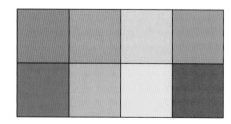

2. Sew 1 **rectangle** to each long edge of Unit 1 to make **Block**. Make 12 Blocks.

Block (make 12)

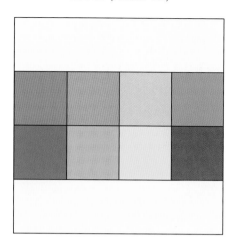

ASSEMBLING THE QUILT TOP

1. Rotating blocks as shown, sew 3 Blocks together to make **Row A**. Make 2 Row A's.

Row A (make 2)

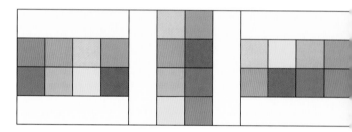

2. Rotating blocks as shown, sew 3 Blocks together to make **Row B**. Make 2 Row B's.

Row B (make 2)

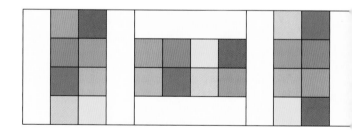

3. Alternating Rows, sew Row A's and Row B's together to make **Quilt Top Center**.
4. Matching centers and corners, sew **side inner borders** to Quilt Top Center. Repeat to sew **top and bottom inner borders** to Quilt Top Center.
5. In the same manner, sew **side outer borders** to Quilt Top and then sew **top** and **bottom outer borders** to Quilt Top.

COMPLETING THE QUILT

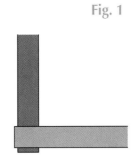
Fig. 1

Follow **Quilting**, page 33, to mark, layer, and quilt as desired. Quilt shown is quilted with an all-over meandering pattern.

Follow **Making a Hanging Sleeve**, page 35, if a hanging sleeve is desired.

To piece binding strips, use the diagonal seams method *(Fig. 1)*.

Matching wrong sides and raw edges, press strip in half lengthwise to complete binding.

Follow **Attaching Binding**, page 36, to bind quilt.

lafayette square

Finished Quilt Size: 64" x 73" (163 cm x 185 cm)
Finished Block Size: 9" x 9" (23 cm x 23 cm)

SHOPPING LIST

Yardage is based on 43"/44" (109 cm/112 cm) wide fabric with a usable width of 40" (102 cm). Charm squares are 5" x 5" (13 cm x 13 cm).

- ☐ One Charm Pack or 42 squares 5" x 5" (13 cm x 13 cm)
- ☐ 1¹/₈ yds (1 m) **each** of green polka dot print, green/black print, and typewriter key print fabric for blocks
- ☐ 1³/₄ yds (1.6 m) of large number print fabric for blocks and outer borders
- ☐ ³/₈ yd (34 cm) of mottled black print fabric for inner borders
- ☐ 4¹/₂ yds (4.1 m) of fabric for backing
- ☐ ⁵/₈ yd (57 m) of fabric for binding
- ☐ 72" x 81" (183 cm x 206 cm) piece of batting

CUTTING THE PIECES

*Follow **Rotary Cutting**, page 31, to cut fabric. Cut all strips from the selvage-to-selvage width of the fabric. Borders are cut exact length. All measurements include $1/4$" seam allowances.*

From large number print fabric:
- Cut 2 **side outer borders** $4^1/2$" x $64^1/2$", pieced as needed.
- Cut 2 **top/bottom outer borders** $4^1/2$" x $63^1/2$", pieced as needed.

From mottled black print fabric:
- Cut 2 **side inner borders** 1" x $63^1/2$", pieced as needed.
- Cut 2 **top/bottom inner borders** 1" x $55^1/2$", pieced as needed.

From fabric for binding:
- Cut 8 **binding strips** $2^1/4$" wide.

MAKING THE BLOCKS

*Follow **Machine Piecing** and **Pressing**, page 32, to make quilt top. Use $1/4$" seam allowances throughout.*

There are 4 different Blocks used in this quilt. Each Block is made from matching fabric strips sewn to the sides of a charm square. The Blocks vary by the width and placement of the strips.

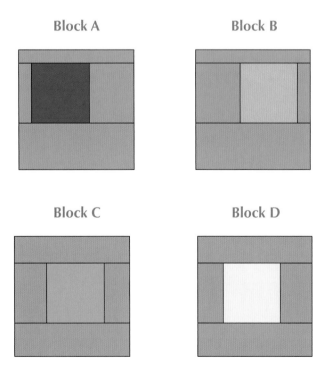

Block A   Block B

Block C   Block D

Make a total of 42 Blocks.

For each **Block A** and **B**, cut 1 **strip** each $1^1/2$" x 5", 4" x 5", $1^1/2$" x $9^1/2$", and 4" x $9^1/2$" from 1 block fabric. Sew strips to sides of a charm square. Block A and B differ in the placement of the 2 smallest strips.

For each **Block C** and **D**, cut 1 **strip** each $2^1/2$" x 5", 3" x 5", $2^1/2$" x $9^1/2$", and 3" x $9^1/2$" from 1 block fabric. Sew strips to sides of a charm square. Block C and D differ in the placement of the 2 smallest strips.

ASSEMBLING THE QUILT TOP CENTER

1. Rotating Blocks as desired, sew 6 Blocks together to make a **Row**. Make 7 Rows.

Row (make 7)

2. Sew Rows together to make Quilt Top Center.
3. Matching centers and corners, sew **side inner borders** to Quilt Top Center. Repeat to sew **top** and **bottom inner borders** to Quilt Top Center.
4. In same manner, sew **side outer borders** to Quilt Top Sew **top** and **bottom outer borders** to Quilt Top

COMPLETING THE QUILT

1. Follow **Quilting**, page 33, to mark, layer, and quilt as desired. Quilt shown is quilted with an all-over meandering pattern.
2. Follow **Making a Hanging Sleeve**, page 35, if a hanging sleeve is desired.
3. To piece binding strips, use the diagonal seams method *(Fig. 1)*.

Fig. 1

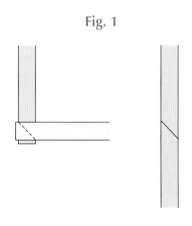

Matching wrong sides and raw edges, press strip in half lengthwise to complete binding.

5. Follow **Attaching Binding**, page 36, to bind quilt.

nest and feathers

Finished Quilt Size: 55" x 72½" (140 cm x 184 cm)
Finished Block Size: 16" x 16" (41 cm x 41 cm)

SHOPPING LIST

Yardage is based on 43"/44" (109 cm/112 cm) wide fabric with a usable width of 40" (102 cm). Fat quarters are approximately 22" x 18" (56 cm x 46 cm).

- ☐ 2 fat quarters **each** of 9 assorted print fabrics for blocks
- ☐ 1 yd (91 cm) of brown solid fabric for sashings
- ☐ 4½ yds (4.1 m) of fabric for backing
- ☐ ½ yd (46 cm) of fabric for binding
- ☐ 63" x 80½" (160 cm x 204 cm) piece of batting

CUTTING THE PIECES

*Follow **Rotary Cutting**, page 31, to cut fabric. When cutting from yardage, cut all strips from the selvage-to-selvage width of the fabric. When cutting from fat quarters, cut all strips parallel to one long edge. Borders and sashings are cut exact length. All measurements include ¹/₄" seam allowances.*

From *each* set of 2 matching fat quarters:
- Cut 4 strips 6" x 22". Cut each strip into 3 **squares** 6" x 6" for a total of 12 squares from **each** of the 9 print fabrics.

From brown solid fabric:
- Cut 3 strips 1¹/₂" wide. From these strips, cut 6 **narrow sashings** 1¹/₂" x 16¹/₂".
- Cut 2 strips 2" wide. From these strips, cut 4 **wide sashings** 2" x 16¹/₂".
- Cut 3 **horizontal sashings** 2" x 51¹/₂", pieced as needed.
- Cut 2 **side borders** 2" x 72", pieced as needed.
- Cut 2 **top/bottom borders** 2" x 51¹/₂", pieced as needed.

From fabric for binding:
- Cut 7 **binding strips** 2¹/₄" wide.

MAKING THE BLOCKS

*Follow **Machine Piecing** and **Pressing**, page 32, to make quilt top. Use ¹/₄" seam allowances throughout.*

1. Using 1 square from each fabric, arrange and sew 9 squares together as desired to make **Unit 1**. (**Note:** Center square will become the smallest square when assembled. Arrange squares with that in mind.) Arranging squares as desired, make 12 Unit 1's.

Unit 1 (make 12)

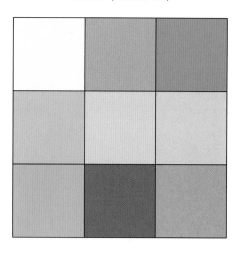

2. Refer to **Fig. 1** to cut Unit 1 along the vertical and horizontal centers to make 4 **Unit 2's**.

Fig. 1

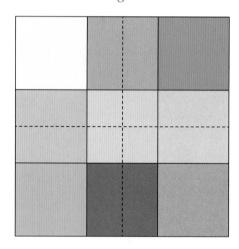

Unit 2

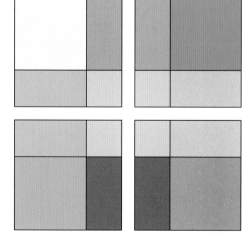

Arrange 4 Unit 2's and sew together to make **Block A**.

Block A

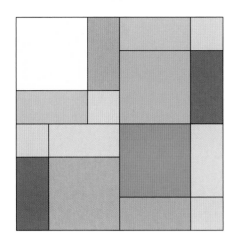

Repeat Steps 2-3 to make a total of 10 Block A's. Repeat Step 2 to arrange 2 Unit 2's and sew together to make Block B. Make 4 **Block B's**.

Block B (make 4)

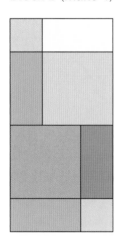

SSEMBLING THE QUILT TOP

Sew 2 Block A's, 2 Block B's and 3 **narrow sashings** together to make **Row 1**. Repeat to make **Row 3**.

Rows 1 and 3

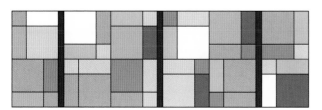

2. Sew 3 Block A's and 2 **wide sashings** together to make **Row 2**. Repeat to make **Row 4**.

Rows 2 and 4

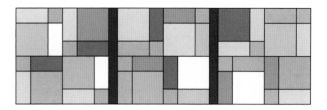

3. Sew Rows 1-4 and 3 **horizontal sashings** together.
4. Matching centers and corners, sew **top** and **bottom borders** to quilt top. Repeat to sew **side borders** to quilt top.

COMPLETING THE QUILT

1. Follow **Quilting**, page 33, to mark, layer, and quilt as desired. Quilt shown is quilted with an all-over meandering pattern.
2. Follow **Making a Hanging Sleeve**, page 35, if a hanging sleeve is desired.
3. To piece binding strips, use the diagonal seams method *(Fig. 2)*.

Fig. 2

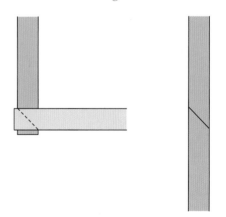

4. Matching wrong sides and raw edges, press strip in half lengthwise to complete binding.
5. Follow **Attaching Binding**, page 36, to bind quilt.

general instructions

To make your quilting easier and more enjoyable, we encourage you to carefully read all of the general instructions, study the color photographs, and familiarize yourself with the individual project instructions before beginning a project.

ABRICS

LECTING FABRICS

oose high-quality, medium-weight 100% cotton rics. All-cotton fabrics hold a crease better, fray less, d are easier to quilt than cotton/polyester blends.

rdage requirements listed for each project are based 43"/44" wide fabric with a "usable" width of 40" after inkage and trimming selvages. Actual usable width ll probably vary slightly from fabric to fabric. Our commended yardage lengths should be adequate for casional re-squaring of fabric when many cuts are quired.

REPARING FABRICS

e-washing fabrics may cause edges to ravel. As a sult, your pre-cut fabric pieces may not be large ough to cut all of the pieces required for your chosen oject. Therefore, we do not recommend pre-washing ur yardage or pre-cut fabrics. Before cutting, prepare rics with a steam iron set on cotton and starch or zing. The starch or sizing will give the fabric a crisp ish. This will make cutting more accurate and may ake piecing easier.

OTARY CUTTING
UTTING FROM YARDAGE

Place fabric on work surface with fold closest to you.

Cut all strips from the selvage-to-selvage width of the fabric unless otherwise indicated in project instructions.

Square left edge of fabric using rotary cutter and rulers *(Figs. 1-2)*.

Fig. 1

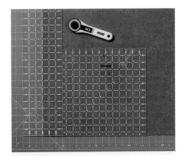

Fig. 2

- To cut each strip required for a project, place ruler over cut edge of fabric, aligning desired marking on ruler with cut edge; make cut *(Fig. 3)*.

Fig. 3

- When cutting several strips from a single piece of fabric, it is important to make sure that cuts remain at a perfect right angle to the fold; square fabric as needed.

CUTTING FROM FAT QUARTERS

- Place fabric flat on work surface with lengthwise (short) edge closest to you.

- Cut all strips parallel to the long edge of the fabric in the same manner as cutting from yardage.

- To cut each strip required for a project, place ruler over cut edge of fabric, aligning desired marking on ruler with cut edge; make cut.

MACHINE PIECING

Precise cutting, followed by accurate piecing, will ensure that all pieces of quilt top fit together well.

- Set sewing machine stitch length for approximately 11 stitches per inch.

- Use neutral-colored general-purpose sewing thread (not quilting thread) in needle and in bobbin.

- An accurate 1/4" seam allowance is *essential*. Presser feet that are 1/4" wide are available for most sewing machines.

- When piecing, always place pieces right sides together and match raw edges; pin if necessary.

- Chain piecing saves time and will usually result in more accurate piecing.

- Trim away points of seam allowances that extend beyond edges of sewn pieces.

SEWING STRIP SETS

When there are several strips to assemble into a strip set, first sew strips together into pairs, then sew pairs together to form strip set. To help avoid distortion, sew seams in opposite directions *(Fig. 4)*.

Fig. 4

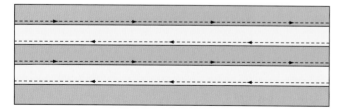

SEWING ACROSS SEAM INTERSECTIONS

When sewing across intersection of two seams, place pieces right sides together and match seams exactly, making sure seam allowances are pressed in opposite directions *(Fig. 5)*.

Fig. 5

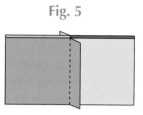

SEWING SHARP POINTS

To ensure sharp points when joining triangular or diagonal pieces, stitch across the center of the "X" (shown in pink) formed on wrong side by previous seam *(Fig. 6)*.

Fig. 6

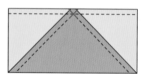

PRESSING

- Use steam iron set on "Cotton" for all pressing.

- Press after sewing each seam.

- Seam allowances are almost always pressed to one side, usually toward darker fabric. However, to reduce bulk it may occasionally be necessary to press seam allowances toward the lighter fabric or even to press them open.

- To prevent dark fabric seam allowance from showing through light fabric, trim darker seam allowance slightly narrower than lighter seam allowance.

- To press long seams, such as those in long strip sets, without curving or other distortion, lay strips across width of the ironing board.

- When sewing blocks into rows, seam allowances may be pressed in one direction in odd numbered rows and in the opposite direction in even numbered rows. When sewing rows together, press seam allowances in one direction.

QUILTING

*Quilting holds the three layers (top, batting, and backing) of the quilt together and can be done by hand or machine. Because marking, layering, and quilting are interrelated and may be done in different orders depending on circumstances, please read entire **Quilting** section, pages 33-35, before beginning project.*

TYPES OF QUILTING DESIGNS

In the Ditch Quilting
Quilting along seamlines or along edges of appliquéd pieces is called "in the ditch" quilting. This type of quilting should be done on side **opposite** seam allowance and does not have to be marked.

Outline Quilting
Quilting a consistent distance, usually ¼", from seam or appliqué is called "outline" quilting. Outline quilting may be marked, or ¼" masking tape may be placed along seamlines for quilting guide. (Do not leave tape on quilt longer than necessary, since it may leave an adhesive residue.)

Motif Quilting
Quilting a design, such as a feathered wreath, is called "motif" quilting. This type of quilting should be marked before basting quilt layers together.

Echo Quilting
Quilting that follows the outline of an appliquéd or pieced design with two or more parallel lines is called "echo" quilting. This type of quilting does not need to be marked.

Channel Quilting
Quilting with straight, parallel lines is called "channel" quilting. This type of quilting may be marked or stitched using a guide.

Crosshatch Quilting
Quilting straight lines in a grid pattern is called "crosshatch" quilting. Lines may be stitched parallel to edges of quilt or stitched diagonally. This type of quilting may be marked or stitched using a guide.

Meandering Quilting
Quilting in random curved lines and swirls is called "meandering" quilting. Quilting lines should not cross or touch each other. This type of quilting does not need to be marked.

Stipple Quilting
Meandering quilting that is very closely spaced is called "stipple" quilting. Stippling will flatten the area quilted and is often stitched in background areas to raise appliquéd or pieced designs. This type of quilting does not need to be marked.

MARKING QUILTING LINES
Quilting lines may be marked using fabric marking pencils, chalk markers, or water- or air-soluble pens.

Simple quilting designs may be marked with chalk or chalk pencil after basting. A small area may be marked, then quilted, before moving to next area to be marked. Intricate designs should be marked before basting using a more durable marker.

Caution: Pressing may permanently set some marks. **Test** different markers **on scrap fabric** to find one that marks clearly and can be thoroughly removed.

A wide variety of pre-cut quilting stencils, as well as entire books of quilting patterns, are available. Using a stencil makes it easier to mark intricate or repetitive designs.

To make a stencil from a pattern, center template plastic over pattern and use a permanent marker to trace pattern onto plastic. Use a craft knife with single or double blade to cut channels along traced lines *(Fig. 7)*.

Fig. 7

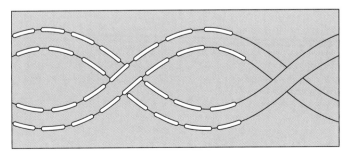

PREPARING THE BACKING

To allow for slight shifting of quilt top during quilting, backing should be approximately 4" larger on all sides. Yardage requirements listed for quilt backings are calculated for 43"/44"w fabric. Using 90"w or 108"w fabric for the backing of a bed-sized quilt may eliminate piecing. To piece a backing using 43"/44"w fabric, use the following instructions.

1. Measure length and width of quilt top; add 8" to each measurement.
2. If determined width is 79" or less, cut backing fabric into two lengths slightly longer than determined *length* measurement. Trim selvages. Place lengths with right sides facing and sew long edges together, forming tube *(Fig. 8)*. Match seams and press along one fold *(Fig. 9)*. Cut along pressed fold to form single piece *(Fig. 10)*.

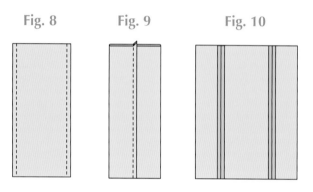

| Fig. 8 | Fig. 9 | Fig. 10 |

3. If determined width is more than 79", it may require less fabric yardage if the backing is pieced horizontally. Divide determined *length* measurement by 40" to determine how many widths will be needed. Cut required number of widths the determined *width* measurement. Trim selvages. Sew long edges together to form single piece.
4. Trim backing to size determined in Step 1; press seam allowances open.

CHOOSING THE BATTING

The appropriate batting will make quilting easier. For fine hand quilting, choose low-loft batting. All cotton or cotton/polyester blend battings work well for machine quilting because the cotton helps "grip" quilt layers. If quilt is to be tied, a high-loft batting, sometimes called extra-loft or fat batting, may be used to make quilt "fluffy."

Types of batting include cotton, polyester, wool, cotton polyester blend, cotton/wool blend, and silk.

When selecting batting, refer to package labels for characteristics and care instructions. Cut batting same size as prepared backing.

ASSEMBLING THE QUILT

1. Examine wrong side of quilt top closely; trim any seam allowances and clip any threads that may show through front of the quilt. Press quilt top, being careful not to "set" any marked quilting lines.
2. Place backing *wrong* side up on flat surface. Use masking tape to tape edges of backing to surface. Place batting on top of backing fabric. Smooth batting gently, being careful not to stretch or tear. Center quilt top *right* side up on batting.
3. Use 1" rustproof safety pins to "pin-baste" all layers together, spacing pins approximately 4" apart. Begin at center and work toward outer edges to secure all layers. If possible, place pins away from areas that will be quilted, although pins may be removed as needed when quilting.

MACHINE QUILTING METHODS

e general-purpose thread in bobbin. Do not use
ilting thread. Thread the needle of machine with
neral-purpose thread or transparent monofilament
ead to make quilting blend with quilt top fabrics. Use
corative thread, such as a metallic or contrasting-color
neral-purpose thread, to make quilting lines stand out
ore.

aight-Line Quilting

*e term "straight-line" is somewhat deceptive, since
rves (especially gentle ones) as well as straight lines
n be stitched with this technique.*

Set stitch length for six to ten stitches per inch and
attach walking foot to sewing machine.

Determine which section of quilt will have longest
continuous quilting line, oftentimes area from center
top to center bottom. Roll up and secure each edge
of quilt to help reduce the bulk, keeping fabrics
smooth. Smaller projects may not need to be rolled.
Begin stitching on longest quilting line, using very
short stitches for the first 1/4" to "lock" quilting.
Stitch across project, using one hand on each side
of walking foot to slightly spread fabric and to guide
fabric through machine. Lock stitches at end of
quilting line.

Continue machine quilting, stitching longer quilting
lines first to stabilize quilt before moving on to other
areas.

Free-Motion Quilting

*Free-motion quilting may be free form or may follow a
marked pattern.*

1. Attach darning foot to sewing machine and lower or
cover feed dogs.
2. Position quilt under darning foot; lower foot. Holding
top thread, take a stitch and pull bobbin thread to
top of quilt. To "lock" beginning of quilting line, hold
top and bobbin threads while making three to five
stitches in place.
3. Use one hand on each side of darning foot to
slightly spread fabric and to move fabric through
the machine. Even stitch length is achieved by using
smooth, flowing hand motion and steady machine
speed. Slow machine speed and fast hand movement
will create long stitches. Fast machine speed and
slow hand movement will create short stitches. Move
quilt sideways, back and forth, in a circular motion,
or in a random motion to create desired designs;
do not rotate quilt. Lock stitches at end of each
quilting line.

MAKING A HANGING SLEEVE

*Attaching a hanging sleeve to the back of a quilt before
the binding is added allows the project to be displayed
on a wall.*

1. Measure width of quilt top edge and subtract 1". Cut
piece of fabric 7"w by determined measurement.
2. Press short edges of fabric piece 1/4" to wrong side;
press edges 1/4" to wrong side again and machine
stitch in place.
3. Matching wrong sides, fold piece in half lengthwise
to form tube.
4. Follow project instructions to sew binding to
quilt top and to trim backing and batting. Before
Blindstitching binding to backing, match raw edges
and stitch hanging sleeve to center top edge on back
of quilt.
5. Finish binding quilt, treating hanging sleeve as part
of backing.
6. Blindstitch bottom of hanging sleeve to backing,
taking care not to stitch through to front of quilt.
7. Insert dowel or slat into hanging sleeve.

ATTACHING BINDING

1. Beginning with one end near center on bottom edge of quilt, lay binding around quilt to make sure that seams in binding will not end up at a corner. Adjust placement if necessary. Matching raw edges of binding to raw edge of quilt top, pin binding to right side of quilt along one edge.

2. When you reach first corner, mark ¹/₄" from corner of quilt top *(Fig. 11)*.

Fig. 11

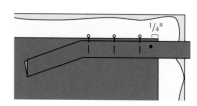

3. Beginning approximately 10" from end of binding and using ¹/₄" seam allowance, sew binding to quilt, backstitching at beginning of stitching and at mark *(Fig. 12)*. Lift needle out of fabric and clip thread.

Fig. 12

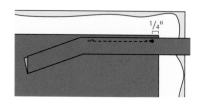

4. Fold binding as shown in **Figs. 13-14** and pin binding to adjacent side, matching raw edges. When you've reached the next corner, mark ¹/₄" from edge of quilt top.

Fig. 13

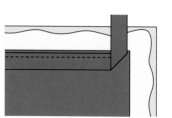

Fig. 14

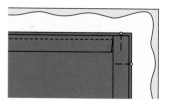

5. Backstitching at edge of quilt top, sew pinned binding to quilt *(Fig. 15)*; backstitch at the next ma Lift needle out of fabric and clip thread.

Fig. 15

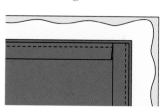

6. Continue sewing binding to quilt, stopping approximately 10" from starting point *(Fig. 16)*.

Fig. 16

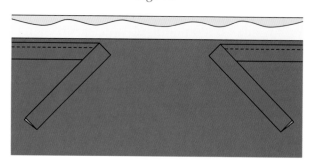

7. Bring beginning and end of binding to center of opening and fold each end back, leaving a ¹/₄" spac between folds *(Fig. 17)*. Finger press folds.

Fig. 17

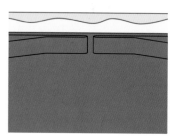

Unfold ends of binding and draw a line across wrong side in finger-pressed crease. Draw a line through the lengthwise pressed fold of binding at the same spot to create a cross mark. With edge of ruler at cross mark, line up 45° angle marking on ruler with one long side of binding. Draw a diagonal line from edge to edge. Repeat on remaining end, making sure that the two diagonal lines are angled the same way *(Fig. 18)*.

Fig. 18

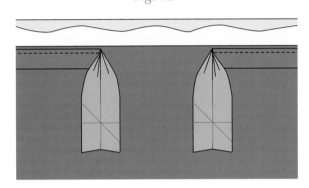

Matching right sides and diagonal lines, pin binding ends together at right angles *(Fig. 19)*.

Fig. 19

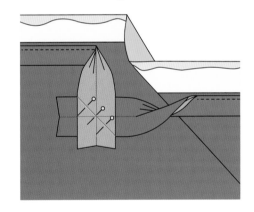

10. Machine stitch along diagonal line *(Fig. 20)*, removing pins as you stitch.

Fig. 20

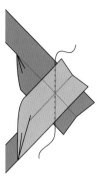

11. Lay binding against quilt to double check that it is correct length.
12. Trim binding ends, leaving 1/4" seam allowance; press seam open. Stitch binding to quilt.
13. Trim backing and batting even with edges of quilt top.
14. On one edge of quilt, fold binding over to quilt backing and pin pressed edge in place, covering stitching line *(Fig. 21)*. On adjacent side, fold binding over, forming a mitered corner *(Fig. 22)*. Repeat to pin remainder of binding in place.

Fig. 21   Fig. 22

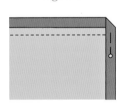 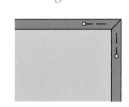

15. Blindstitch binding to backing, taking care not to stitch through to front of quilt.

BLIND STITCH

Come up at 1, go down at 2, and come up at 3 *(Fig. 23)*. Length of stitches may be varied as desired.

Fig. 23

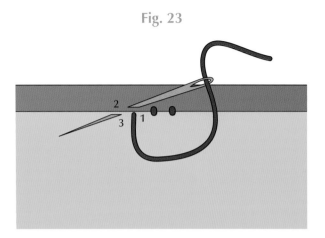

SIGNING AND DATING YOUR QUILT

A completed quilt is a work of art and should be signed and dated. There are many different ways to do this and numerous books on the subject. The label should reflect the style of the quilt, the occasion or person for which it was made, and the quilter's own particular talents. Following are suggestions for recording the history of quilt or adding a sentiment for future generations.

- Embroider quilter's name, date, and any additional information on quilt top or backing. Matching floss such as cream floss on white border, will leave a subtle record. Bright or contrasting floss will make the information stand out.

- Make label from muslin and use permanent marker to write information. Use different colored permanent markers to make label more decorative. Stitch label to back of quilt.

- Use photo-transfer paper to add image to white or cream fabric label. Stitch label to back of quilt.

- Piece an extra block from quilt top pattern to use a label. Add information with permanent fabric pen. Appliqué block to back of quilt.

fabrics used

As we all know, fabrics that are available in stores today may not be available six months from now. Sometimes when fabrics are no longer available in stores they may be available on the internet. For your convenience, we have listed the fabrics used for our quilts below:

An Apple a Day
page 2, was made using Little Apples fabrics by Aneela Hoey for Moda Fabrics.

Backyard Fun
page 8, was made using Backyard Baby fabrics by Patty Sloniger for Michael Miller Fabrics.

Coming Home
page 12, was made using Hometown fabrics by Sweetwater for Moda Fabrics.

Floating 8
page 18, was made using Sorbet fabrics by Michael Miller Fabrics.

Lafayette Square
page 22, was made using Circa 1934 fabrics by Cosmo Cricket for Moda Fabrics.

Nest and Feathers
page 26, was made using Feather n Stitch fabrics by Blend Fabrics.

---

meet the designers

janie lou
QUILT. SEW. CREATE.

…anie lou is a small company …rted by two sisters, Jane Vogl …t) and Jenny Clinard. "Hobbies …t included sewing 'anything …d everything' since we were …ung grew into a passion that …vitably became a business," …e explained. They began … making custom quilts and …ntually opened an online …re and started traveling in … quilt show circuit. Recently they "landed" in St. Louis, …ssouri, and opened their shop to the public.

The new shop reflects the sisters' love of fabric, colors, and design. "We choose fabrics and quilts that we love to love," Jane said. "Our favorite projects are those that make us feel rejuvenated and happy." Their clean, crisp, contemporary designs work with many different fabrics, and the patterns are intended for all levels of quilters. "If you are a busy woman in today's world, our projects give you a creative outlet," Jane said. To learn more about the designers and their shop, visit the janie lou quilts page on Facebook or their website at janielouquilts.com.

Metric Conversion Chart

Inches x 2.54 = centimeters (cm)
Inches x 25.4 = millimeters (mm)
Inches x .0254 = meters (m)

Yards x .9144 = meters (m)
Yards x 91.44 = centimeters (cm)
Centimeters x .3937 = inches (")
Meters x 1.0936 = yards (yd)

Standard Equivalents

1/8"	3.2 mm	0.32 cm	1/8 yard	11.43 cm	0.11 m
1/4"	6.35 mm	0.635 cm	1/4 yard	22.86 cm	0.23 m
3/8"	9.5 mm	0.95 cm	3/8 yard	34.29 cm	0.34 m
1/2"	12.7 mm	1.27 cm	1/2 yard	45.72 cm	0.46 m
5/8"	15.9 mm	1.59 cm	5/8 yard	57.15 cm	0.57 m
3/4"	19.1 mm	1.91 cm	3/4 yard	68.58 cm	0.69 m
7/8"	22.2 mm	2.22 cm	7/8 yard	80 cm	0.8 m
1"	25.4 mm	2.54 cm	1 yard	91.44 cm	0.91 m

Production Team: Technical Writer – Lisa Lancaster; Technical Editors - Frances Huddleston and Jean Lewis; Graphic Artist – Kara Darling, Photography Stylist – Sondra Daniel; Photographer - Ken West.

We have made every effort to ensure that these instructions are accurate and complete. We cannot, however, be responsible for human error, typographical mistakes, or variations in individual work.